The Secret to Breaking

the

B. R. O. K. E. Code

Manifesting Growth, Abundance, and Overflow

Table of Contents

PROLOGUE

Hey You!

Well, today's the day. You're headed to bankruptcy court and a judge will decide if all this is finally coming to an end. You're scared of how it will turn out, but I can tell you it will be okay. You'll walk out of that courtroom in a few hours feeling like you can breathe again.

This is the first day of the rest of your life.

I can't lie, the road back won't be easy. There will be more sacrifices. But a few years from now you'll be better than you've been in a really long time. So you need to just trust the process. You need to trust yourself—which is exactly why I wanted to talk to you.

While you might think that putting the debt behind you will be the hardest part, actually, it's the easiest. The damage that this season of your life has caused was not just to your credit score and that overdrawn checking account. The real damage is so much deeper than that. What you don't realize yet is you're more shaken than you know. Along with that debt, you've been carrying guilt and shame because you think you should have known better. You've always been smart. You've always figured out how to make it happen, how to make it work, how to fix it. But you couldn't this time. And that's okay. Why? Because you just didn't know.

So whenever you feel the urge to beat yourself up, don't you dare do it.

Forgive yourself for not knowing what to do and how to do it.

Forgive yourself for spending too much.

Forgive yourself for being hardheaded and ignoring signs that you were headed for trouble.

Forgive yourself for not being able to see that you deserved so much more.

Let it all go.

You know how you like to play things over and over in your mind. You want to figure out where you went wrong. But you don't have to do that anymore. We're going to fix this; and not only will you come out ahead and far better off than you could have ever dreamed, but you're going to be open about your story and share everything you've learned. You endured all this not just to help yourself and your family, but to help so many other people break free from this bondage, too. You're going to show the masses how to not end up here. You'll teach them how to turn their lives around. You'll help them buy homes, invest, and grow their money. You'll teach them how to plant seeds in fertile soil. You'll help them open their eyes and see more for themselves than they ever imagined was possible. As you soar, so many others will, too.

Alright, girl, I know you need to get to it. This is a big day for you. I hope these words come right on time when you need them most.

Don't ever forget them.

-Constance

INTRODUCTION

I know when you picked up this book and saw my big smile on the cover, you expected that we would start out more happy than heavy. We are supposed to be talking about how to achieve the great things that you desire and deserve—how to finally attract wealth, abundance, and overflow that you want in every aspect of your life, particularly in your finances. And, you're right, we are definitely going to get you moving in the right direction. But this book is not about just earning more money to buy more things. It's about transformation.

And if you know anything about what it takes to truly transform anything in your life, you know change that's deep always begins on the inside. Transformation comes from shifting something on the inside of you. It comes from clearing away blocks that get in the way of greatness and ties that bind you to mistakes you've made and even the person you used to be. It comes from shaking off some stuff—like shame.

Shifting is a spiritual thing.

Now, I didn't intend to take you to church, but regardless of what God or religious practice you follow, chances are you are holding this book because you are ready to shift something in your life. You want something bigger and better for yourself and your family. You know, like I know, that there is so much more out there for you to have and to become. You have dreams that you want to come true and prayers that you want answered. You may want to live in a better neighborhood so you can send your kids to a better school. You want to save for college and retirement. You want to know how it feels to not have to think about having more month than money. You always want there to be more than enough. And you think that if you could just make more, you could have more. But I am here to tell you that it's so much deeper than that. I could tell you three steps to make a million dollars right now, but if you haven't made that shift to understand why you need to keep it, sow it, and grow it—or even why you deserve it in the first place—then it will slip right through your fingers like sand.

The shift starts with forgiving yourself for everything that you feel you've done wrong up until now.

If you've heard me speak about my personal story before, you probably know that I filed bankruptcy. (If you're not familiar with what happened and why, don't worry, we'll get into it in more detail in a few pages.) But my decision to file that paperwork was one of the hardest and best decisions of my life. I'd recklessly spent myself into hundreds upon hundreds of thousands of dollars in debt, and it was a hole so deep that I couldn't work myself out of, no matter how hard I tried. So I needed to do something drastic. For me, that meant walking away from my debt so I could get a clean slate and a chance to rebuild my finances and my life. In the moment, the exhilaration from the process was so emotionally overwhelming that I walked out of the courthouse feeling like my feet weren't even touching the ground. I felt physically lighter. But as I started putting the pieces of my life back together, I started to think about how I got to a point where I was earning over $200K a year but could barely afford gas and groceries. That's when I realized that I wasn't just broke financially, but I was *broken* in many ways.

My mentality around making and spending money—broken.

My perspective on possibilities for my life and people who could shift me—broken.

My openness to knowledge about creating wealth—broken.

My understanding of what I deserved—majorly broken.

My mental and spiritual brokenness was far more detrimental to me than not having any money. In fact, it was the reason *why* I didn't have any.

The words you read in that letter were what I wish I could have said to myself twelve years ago. I couldn't, because I didn't know. But eventually I got to the bottom of what I needed to do to shift my mindset, to let go of my past so I could move fully into my future.

And now I want to share what I've learned with you.

While we'll talk a bit about your money and financial situation in this book, what I want you to understand first is that *broke* is about more than just what you have in your pocket—it's about what you have in your mind. We'll talk about that more than anything else. Once you've shifted your mindset, once you understand how you got here, why you've spent years sitting in struggle and stuck in shame about your life, choices, and money, then, I promise you, you can have, do, and be anything. *Anythin*

YOU HAVE TO BREAK TO BREAK THROUGH

When we talk about breaking the code, we're talking about a breach of behavior that leads to a typical result. Today, you may be living a typical life. A life that is defined by statistics, standards, and maybe even an economic status that limits you. A life that only meets the minimal expectations that some people around you have set for you, based on who they are, what they've done, and how far they've gone. And while you likely want and need more, typical is where you've been trapped for so long because it's easy and comfortable. It's within your reach. It doesn't take extra effort to want what we've always seen and have what we've always had. We can live a typical life with the people we've always known, by living and working in the same place.

But you know, like I know, that you weren't created for typical. You were born for bigger things. You come from a lineage and a legacy of greatness. You are descendants of royalty. Success is your birthright. So that means that you can—and should—have a great life. You can have the booming business or the career of your dreams. You can have the family, the spouse, and the vacations. You can invest and become wealthy so that you can grow money to give back to your community in big ways. You can live and give. This is the life that should be typical for you. To have it, you have to have the courage to break some things. Break habits. Break behaviors. Break beliefs. Break what you've learned about how to live, what you should have, and what's possible. Break other people's expectations of you. Break the generational curses. Break any and everything that keeps you in bondage to the life that you no longer desire to live.

Break it all so you can break through.

WHAT IS THE B.R.O.K.E. CODE?

In case you haven't noticed, we're going to talk a lot about what you need to break in this book, and the courage it takes to do it. And once we identify the limitations that you need to lift and remove from your life, you'll need a blueprint to rebuild and to bring the abundance, growth, and overflow that belongs to you. The blessing is that you are holding that plan in your hands.

The B.R.O.K.E. Code is a set of principles that you can apply to any area of your life and achieve unrecognizable transformation. It doesn't matter if you want more money than you need to improve your quality of life and invest to build wealth, start a business of your dreams, or pave a path to your passion for making a difference in someone else's life; if you take what you learn here and use it, you will see your life significantly shift in your favor.

In Chapter Two, I'll delve deeper into The Code that I've used to create radical results in my own life, so you can see how you can do the same. I'll also give you the specific steps and tools to put it to work. But even before you get there, I want to introduce you to the framework, and encourage you to begin to think about what you need to shift in your life, and the reasons why you haven't, until today, been able to make it happen. This is not a reading-only book. This is a tool that pushes you to action. So we're going to get to work right away. Here's what you need to start thinking about:

Belief: Having anything that you desire begins with believing it can happen. Many of us say that we are believers, we are faithful, and that we trust God for miracles and to do the impossible, but when it comes to wanting something big for ourselves, we don't really believe we can have it. In fact, if we're honest, we don't actually believe we *should* have it.

Let's look at the lie we tell ourselves—

The Lie: There are some things that I can't get in this life because I am too _____ to have it.

But here's the Truth: You are not counted out for being a minority, a woman, born and raised in a poor family, not having a college degree, being too young or too old. The truth is simple. You can and should have everything this world has to offer. You are, by birthright, entitled to it. Success, in the most extraordinary way, is your destiny. Claim it.

The Question:

What do you really want for your life, but don't believe you can ever have? Why do you believe that what you want is not possible for you? Write it below.

_____

_____

_____

_____

Ready: Will Smith is often famously quoted as saying, "So if you stay ready, you ain't gotta get ready." Readiness is the step after belief for a reason. If you really examine why we stay stuck, one of the big reasons is that we are conditioned to want and then wait. If you have ever found the courage to actually ask God for something, I am willing to bet that you asked and then stepped back. If you believe that is what prayer and patience is about, I am here to tell you, right now, you've been wanting and waiting in vain. That is not faith. It's foolishness.

Think about the wide receiver who is expected to catch the ball and run it into the end zone for a touchdown. Does he stand on the field with his arms down, and not lift them until after the quarterback releases the ball?

No.

He's poised and prepared in his position, expecting that ball to come his way.

Once we decide what we want, the next step is to prepare ourselves to receive it. We have to get in position. Good things don't come to those who wait. Good things, and goals, come to those who *walk*. Passivity is no longer your pass to escape the life you see for yourself. It's time to get in the game.

There can be many reasons why you don't feel ready to improve some area of your life. We're going to smash them all—one at a time.

Let's look at the lie we tell ourselves—

The Lie: Yes, I can want things. But what it takes to get them is out of my control.

But here's the Truth: You have the ability, the intelligence, and access to the resources to prepare your mind, spirit, and money for what's coming your way.

The Question:

What are the steps you feel you need to take to get each of the things that you've written down above? Write those down here.

_____

_____

_____

_____

_____

Obsessed: When we want something, I mean *really* want it, there is nothing that can keep us from it. Your goals and dreams require an obsession that is beyond what makes sense, or seems logical or possible. As motivational speaker Eric Thomas says, "When you want to succeed as bad as you want to breathe, you will be successful." That level of commitment is what it takes to get out of poverty. To have a great life. To have a great marriage, business, or career. You have to want it more than you want anything else. Like your life, your children's lives, your next breath depends on it. Radical results require relentless focus. No exceptions or excuses. You have it in you.

Let's look at the lie we tell ourselves—

The Lie: I can't give my dreams and goals my full focus. I have a family, kids, and a job already. I don't have the time or the energy anymore.

But here's the Truth: It's not a myth that we make time for the things we want. When you commit to change, your life and everything in it has no choice but to align.

The Question: What do you need to clear out and change about your lifestyle to make room for extreme focus on what you want? Write it below.

_____

_____

_____

_____

_____

_____

Knowledgeable: Whatever it is you are setting out to do, you'll have to become an expert in it. Period. Know it in and out. Seek information and ideas about the topic. Understand the strategies that have worked for people who've already achieved the goals that you're after. Study. When it comes to knowledge, there is no such thing as too much.

Let's look at the lie we tell ourselves—

The Lie: It's too late for me to learn anything new.

But here's the Truth: Life is constantly about learning and applying new information. Knowledge is your key to moving out of struggle and scarcity and into your abundance and overflow. You have to start growing. Feed your mind what it needs to flourish and watch everything you touch do the same.

The Question: What specific knowledge do I need to acquire to get what I want? Write your thoughts below.

_____

_____

_____

_____

_____

_____

Economical: Finances will play a big part in your plan. To get more, you will have to give up more. You will have to stop spending every dime that comes into your checking account. To be in position for opportunities means that you may have to get into rooms. You may have to pay for tools and technology you need to build the business or textbooks to get the degree or learn a new trade. If you manage what you have well, there will always be more.

Let's look at the lie we tell ourselves—

The Lie: I can't save any money. I have just enough to pay my bills and there is no extra for anything else.

But here's the Truth: This is about doing what you've never done before. If you've struggled with managing money all your life, it's because you haven't been taught how and it's never really been required. So many of us (myself included) have had to learn financial principles from the ground up as adults, but there is no way to create the results that you want in your life without getting control over your money. Dreams demand discipline. Be willing to sacrifice for your success.

The Questions:

How much money will you need to get to your goal? Write it down.

_____

_____

_____

_____

_____

_____

What can you cut out of your life to start saving more? Write your thoughts below.

_____

_____

_____

_____

_____

_____

The actions that you'll take while reading this book, and hopefully after, will have more meaning when they are attached to something you want, a vision that you see for yourself and for your life. If you took the time to think through the questions above, you should be clear about the desires you have for your life and what you need to turn those dreams into realities.

Now, let's dig into the work to make your someday into your *today*.

START AND DON'T EVER STOP

One more thing. From this point forward, I want you to stop thinking about and focusing on everything you don't have. It doesn't matter where you are with your life, your money, or what bad mistakes you've made. This is about a fresh start. It's about facing hard things so you can fix them. You can become the person that you've always wished and wanted to be. Successful. Wealthy. In control of your day-to-day life, your dreams, and your destiny. All of that can happen for you. Yes, *you*. Believe that.

Throughout this book, I'll share some of my personal story as a catalyst to encourage and equip you to take intentional action. But what I want you know, above all else, is that I am just girl from San Jose, California who figured out how to turn a little into a lot. I wasn't sent out into the world with a plan for my life, other than to survive. I don't have a post-secondary education. I didn't have a guide for anything that I've ever achieved.

What I did have was a will to win. I started, I stumbled, I fell, and I failed. But I got up, and I kept going. I *keep* going.

The two hardest things you will ever have to do in this life are decide to start and decide to keep going. If you can do that, if you motivate yourself to move one day, everything else will feel easy. Make today that day.

CHAPTER ONE
BREAKING THE CYCLE OF POVERTY

"Then when you know better, do better." – Maya Angelou

People who have met me in the last ten, maybe fifteen, years of my life sometimes find it hard to believe the journey I've had to take to get to this place in my life. The journey has been amazing. Not amazing because it was perfect; in fact, quite the contrary. It has been the imperfections, the bumps in the road, and overcoming seemingly impossible situations that have truly made my journey so worthwhile and rewarding. I sit here today, CEO of Catalyst Real Estate Professionals, the largest African American-owned real estate firm in northern California. A best-selling author, an investor with a diverse portfolio, a coach, a speaker, a mentor, and a mentee. I have had the distinct honor of being featured in several national publications like *Black Enterprise*, *Huffington Post*, and *Rolling Out Magazine.* By far, the accomplishment I am the most proud of is being the wife of Warren Carter, who I've been with since I was 15 years old, and being the mother to my 4 beautiful and amazing kids. We are forever grateful for the great village of support and unwavering love that surrounds us. Yes... Life is good.

Like many of us who grew up with parents and families who may have lacked the knowledge, money, or tools to set their children up for success, I had to figure life out fast and on my own, and those early adult years were far from pretty. It's no surprise that I made so many mistakes. And while we all know that struggle sometimes supersedes success, what we often forget is that our first choices in life, the ones that have the power to determine the trajectory of who we are and what we become, are dictated more by the examples we have in our homes. Our environment, our role models and their attitudes around growth, wealth, and success influence us in ways that we don't realize.

Our mistakes aren't always a result of knowing what to do and choosing another action or route. Usually, our mistakes start with mimicking what we've seen, which becomes what we know.

Both of my parents were born and raised in a small, relatively unknown town in Arkansas. They grew up extremely poor, and, like many of their generation, lived a "just-enough-to-get-by" life. My father attended school for the first time at eight years old after a stranger threw a box of clothes for him to wear in his family's front yard. Growing up, I'd listen to him tell stories about how little his family had. I knew that scarcity shaped his mindset and it was manifested in many of the struggles as well as principles we were taught and had growing up. The pride he had with making something great out of very little showed up in many ways. On any given day, he'd recall everything from not being able to attend school until he was eight years old because his mother, who we called Madear, couldn't afford clothes for him to wear, to playing outside with his only toy, a red, rusty Tonka truck with no wheels that he pulled around with a string. His childhood was one of wearing his grown uncle's hand-me-downs when he was just an adolescent.

My mother, on the other hand, still grew up in poor, but just a little bit better off. Her mom, who we also call Madear, was a widow and the mother of 11 children. She picked cotton for a living, and while she earned little money, she was known for keeping her kids clean, well fed, and nicely dressed. There was nothing left for frills, but her children had what they needed. It also helped that by the time my mother was born, many of her older siblings were grown and had moved out of the house, and some had already started families of their own. The older children always made sure that Madear and the younger siblings were taken care of.

My parents met as teenagers. Mom was 16 when she and my dad had my oldest brother. After graduating from high school, my father was drafted in the Army, but chose to join the Marine Corp and went straight to Vietnam, serving on the front lines. When he returned home a couple of years later as a Corporal and decorated war hero, he was stationed in California. My mother soon followed, and they were married just shortly before having my sister. A naïve eighteen-year-old-girl and a young boy who became a man on a battlefield were thrust into adulthood, suddenly having to figure out how to raise children, keep a roof over their heads, and find jobs to support their growing family. They were children raising children. And their relationship didn't stand a chance under all that pressure. Fighting. Financial instability. Dysfunction. It was a constant cycle that continued throughout their entire marriage, and each time my parents would break up and get back together (which happened every other year after my sister was born), a piece was torn out of our already too-fragile family unit. I didn't realize it then, but so much of what we thought about marriage, money, and how couples work out conflict was shaped during those years. When I entered the picture five years later, my parents' relationship was still pretty rocky. I remember being shuffled from house to house, wondering why we all couldn't stay together. Despite what I saw, I knew what a family was "supposed" to be. I knew we should all be in one house, and while other little girls only dreamed about pink bikes and Barbies, what I wished for was having me, my mom, my dad, brother, and sister in one place, happy. I didn't understand why I couldn't see my dad every day or why my mom didn't come home. As confusing as it all was, I never doubted their love for me. What we didn't have in money, my parents made up for in love. I was kissed, hugged, and celebrated every day. I was told that I was special and smart by them and everyone else in my family. I felt secure despite the chaos. Stability still felt like a mom, dad, and kids in a house of their own. Watching television together. Holidays. Dancing and singing. Birthdays. That's what I wanted. In the subconscious of my six-year-old mind, there was probably a part of me that thought if my parents could just stay in the same house, that could fix everything and maybe they wouldn't separate again.

At age six, I finally got exactly what I wanted. We moved to a three-bedroom home on Flickinger Avenue—all five of us. My dream to have my mom, dad, and siblings all under one roof had come true. Always willing to give someone else a hand-up, my parents agreed to allow an old friend to stay with us for a while. Our small house became even smaller with an extra person squeezed in, and it wasn't bad until a cousin and an auntie moved in, too. Then another cousin. Then a second aunt and her family of four, soon followed by one more cousin and her husband. At one point, we had 19 people living in a three-bedroom house that was meant for a family of five. It was as if word got out that my mom and dad hit the lotto, got rich, and were all of a sudden in a position to take care of everybody they knew. It was a madhouse.

There was constant partying and anything else you can imagine went down in that house. My parents were busy working odd hours most of the time, so they didn't partake too much in the shenanigans. Nevertheless, the house was wild, and I was exposed to a lot of things a little girl shouldn't have been exposed to. Things that my eight-year-old mind could in no way ever understand.

Fortunately, when I turned ten my parents got fed up with all the chaos and shenanigans and moved our family into a condo that was just big enough for our family. Life was pretty fun. My family is hilarious! We love to laugh and joke, so I enjoyed coming home from school. I loved being around my mom and dad, watching TV or making up dances and rapping with my sister and cousins. It was always funny listening to my mom curse and watching my dad cringe and shake his head and laugh. Around that time, he became a born-again Christian and was a deeply involved Deacon at my uncle's church. My parents were complete opposites, but they truly did love one another. As my dad took on more responsibilities at the church and got deeply "religious" they started to grow apart.

My mother left our home for good when I was 14. I remember the day she left. It devastated my family. I came home from spending the night at my cousin's house and what was normally a fun and vibrant home was now a cold and gloomy house. I couldn't put my finger on it, but there was definitely a shift of "light" energy. It wasn't too long after I got home when my dad told me my mother decided to move out. My sister and I secretly knew that she was having an affair, but we never thought she would actually leave. Over time, I would hear my dad praying for her, asking the Lord to touch her heart. In spite of the prayers, and all the hoping and wishing from my siblings and I, she never came back home. When she left, she was gone for good. At times, I felt as though she had literally forgotten she had children. She believed her young teenage children were grown, and because of that belief, she went on to live her life. There was very little, if any, communication between us, and she contributed nothing financially. I was so lost, angry, and confused. I would write in my journal about how she made me feel; writing was the only outlet I had at the time that allowed me to express my feelings. She moved through life seemingly without a care in the world, but I was only 14—by today's standards, still a child. A vulnerable little girl who still really needed her mother.

My dad was the most consistent person in my life. He was so loving and caring. He was indeed my Superman. He showed up to every single event I participated in when I was growing up. He'd be front and center, right there in the front row. Every award I received, every concert I played in, every assembly I performed in, my dad would be there with the biggest smile on his face, beaming with pride.

When I was 16, we moved from the condo he was renting, and he bought a house. The house itself was a total wreck, but my dad put all his blood, sweat, and tears into fixing it up himself. Eventually, his hard work paid off and this raggedy house became our home. The next year, I started hanging with a friend who had also moved from my old neighborhood to this one. Her mom was single, and we would somewhat jokingly say things like, "Wouldn't it be cool if my mom and your dad hooked up?" Well, much to our surprise, that is exactly what happened. I really didn't know much about her mom, but once they began dating my friend (her daughter) began sharing with me troubling things about her mom. I would always tell my dad what I had been told, but he never believed me and, to make matters worse, he would go back and tell his girlfriend what was being said. Of course, this angered her, and she'd go back and slap her daughter for telling me.

I remember the day he told my siblings and me he was getting married. He came home one day and said, "Dorothy and I are getting married whether YOU like it or not!" and just like that, only six short months after they met, they were married. There was an immediate change in the positive, loving interaction between my father and me. His wife was very manipulative, and it seemed as if her primary goal in life was to turn my father against me. She didn't approve of the playful banter between my dad and me, and would accuse me of things like being disrespectful. Her oldest daughter would hide my things or bleach my clothes. Eventually, she convinced her other daughters to turn against me, including the daughter who was originally my friend. She hid the fact that she smoked cigarettes and would smoke in the house when he was gone and then lie about it. One day they decided they needed my room and I should be moved into the smaller one. Sad to say, but my dad was such a pushover when it came to her, and anything she said he would do. He came to me one day and said, "Baby, they will respect me if I give them your room; Right now, they don't respect me." My response was, "Dad, they don't respect you now and they will never respect you, but this is your house, do what you gotta do." On the day they decided to relocate me into the smaller room, I was out with a couple of friends. When I came home, I was in complete shock to see what they had done to my personal belongings. They threw away everything they could not fit into the smaller room. My mementos, yearbooks, old photos, and keepsakes

I had kept since elementary school were all gone. My clothes were in the trash, my headboard was in the garage. This was such a complete, and total disrespect and violation of all my personal belongings. I was in disbelief at how not only my things were being discarded, but how I was being treated. It literally broke my heart and brought me to tears. My dad's wife got angry at my response, walked out, and slammed the door behind her. My dad, in turn, got upset with me, and it was clearer than ever that my feelings were no longer a factor in any of his decision making. Soon after, my dad would say to me the 5 most hurtful words that I ever heard come out of his mouth. He ordered me to "leave and never come back". My heart sank, my soul ached...my dad, my hero...The only person who was consistent in my life threw me out like he'd allowed them to do with all my personal belongings. I was truly alone in every sense of the word. I was on my own with no place to go. I would couch surf at different friends' homes, but that only lasted for so long. My friends were still living with their parents, and at some point, their parents wanted to know what was going on and why I was there. I would sometimes spend the night at my then-boyfriend Warren's house, but like all the other parents, his wondered what was going on as well. Some nights I had no other options and would just sleep in my car. This was my life for a while. Eventually, Warren and I saved a little money, and my future husband and I got our first apartment together.

I worked various jobs, starting at HP as a Security Guard. Over time I worked my way up to an IT Analyst. Warren and I got married when I was 22 and he was 24. We had our first daughter the next year and purchased our first home a few months later. Life was good, hard but good. We were happy. The first day we stayed in our new home, which was an hour and a half away from all our friends, family, and familiarity, a sense of regret came over me. I remember thinking, *what did we do?* Life as we knew it had changed. The year leading up to this, we'd been living in an apartment next door to my sister, walking distance from my brother, and around the corner from my father. We were so far away from our village and security. Ready or not, we were adults. Me, him, and baby girl, we had no one to depend on except each other. There were lots of highs and lows, from losing jobs to living in the land of NSFs to almost losing our home. I was commuting four hours a day to my job in Palo Alto, missing out on the life that we were working so hard to create, always striving to be better than we were the day, the week, the month before. My daughter was growing, and I was missing her milestones. This beautiful home that we bought was bigger than any home that both Warren and I had ever lived in. I hardly got to enjoy it or spend time in it. Again, I spent four hours commuting every single day.

One day, I decided that I would try my hand in real estate. I loved the process of buying my home, although it was to date the worst business experience I had ever had. I loved the sense of accomplishment, hope, and security we had in homeownership. I wanted other people like me to experience the same thing, even more than that I wanted to protect people from experiencing what I had when I went through the process.

I would see billboards of real estate companies offering real estate classes with the promise to train new agents. I scheduled appointments with a couple of brokers. I told them my dreams and aspirations of becoming a real estate agent and helping people like me become homeowners. Two of the brokers I met with almost had the exact same response: "You work for HP, why would you want to leave your job security, and retirement, and benefits for a career like this? You won't be as successful; you should keep your day job." After the second broker told me this, I got discouraged. I decided to keep working. I was good at having a J-O-B and would often work my way up to better jobs at better companies with better pay. However, real estate was still there, something I still wanted to pursue if and when the opportunity presented itself. Family and friends would watch my journey, and they also would be inspired to create their own dream of homeownership, and I would always guide them through the process. I knew this stuff, I knew I could do it. One day the need to pursue my real estate dream overtook me, and I decided it was time. I began the pursuit of getting my license in real estate. I thought I would dabble on the side and make some extra money while working my full-time job, but just as I was finishing up my licensing, I received the news that I would be laid off at Cisco Systems. I would get a little bit of a severance package plus unemployment. I thought to myself, *this is the perfect opportunity to dive head first into this real estate thing. Not just dip my feet in, but get my whole body immersed in real estate.* About a month after my layoff, I passed the real estate exam. With no clients and nowhere to start, I began learning as much as I could about the business. I took class after class and implemented just about every technique I learned. Some worked, and some didn't. I had to figure out for myself what would be my best method of building a successful business. It wasn't easy, but it was necessary. As soon as I passed the exam, I sent out this email to everyone I knew:

-----Original Message-----
From: Constance Smith
[SMTP:constance_smith@yahoo.com]
Sent: Wednesday, October 09, 2002 10:07 AM
To: constancecarter@attbi.com
Subject: Buying or Selling a Home

Hi Friends,
I just want to let you all know that I just got my Real Estate License and I would like to help you buy or sell your home. The reason that I chose to get into this field is that I want to help people reach their dreams. I want to help people who never thought they could own a home, own one. If you're in the market for a home, either buying or selling, please let me know.
-Constance

"Help" has been the center of my business from the very beginning. I'm not the best salesperson, but because my business has always been about serving and helping others, I've been able to help thousands, and have built a successful business because of it.

Starting off, we had two old, beat-up cars, and I drove one of them—a Pontiac Sunfire with a faded hood and ripped-up seats. I was embarrassed about how raggedy that car was, but I knew I had to start somewhere. I started in real estate in January, and didn't make a dime until July. During the last five months of my first year, I made $70,000, and matched my previous annual salary. That was the last year I made less than six figures in my business. I never, ever looked back.

I know you may be thinking that this is the typical rags-to-riches story that you expected. And, in some ways, it is. The harder I worked, the more I made. Money started to come in fast, and it was more cash than I had ever had access to in my life. It felt endless, and so we started spending as if the well would never run dry.

Our first home was a 2100sqft 4-bedroom 3-bathroom home with an office & private retreat. We traded this home that was bigger than all the homes my husband and I had ever lived in our whole lives, for a brand-new, six-bedroom, 3500 sq. ft. home with all the bells and whistles. Suddenly our first home was too small for our family of 3. Spending $30K on landscaping and $100K on upgrades. I'd traded in my beat-up car and eventually got a brand-new Mercedes Benz. These were not things we needed, these were merely wants. We did at least try to make some wise investments with rental properties, but just like a lot of people before the crash, we got stuck with our pants down with these adjustable rate & negative amortization mortgages and couldn't refinance them when the market shifted and ended up foreclosing and short selling.

Within two years, I was bringing in over $200K annually, but with $15K-$20K in monthly expenses, the deposits flew out of our account as fast as they came in.

I had every intention of never being broke again in my life. I'd figured out a formula to make sure I would always have more money than I needed. Working with my real estate clients and seeing the credit and financial challenges that many of them faced when trying to buy homes, I vowed that I would live modestly, beneath my means. I would not spend frivolously, I would have money in the bank, I would keep my credit great, and I would live well.

All of that sounded great, and it would have been. It should have been.

But I was little girl who, in what felt like a blink of an eye, went from having nothing to having everything she could ever want. A girl who watched her parents struggle. A girl who, just ten years before, had been sleeping in her car. A girl who wanted to give her kids all the things that she never had. A girl who wanted to look and live like the success that she worked so hard for.

So that girl became a woman who got in way over her head, and lost everything she worked so hard for. My six-figure salary and ridiculous spending habits put me in an insurmountable mountain of debt, and filing bankruptcy was the only way out. Eventually, I would get back what I lost, and then some. But it was a hard and a humiliating climb back. Fortunately, that hard fall left me with some hard lessons, and when God blessed me and reopened the door to bigger and better opportunities for financial success, I didn't let Him or myself down again.

Knowing better is about doing better.

WE ARE WHAT WE LEARN...AT FIRST

If you see some parallels between my life and yours, good. From homeless to heights that I never could have imagined, only to lose it all, my life has been full of twists and turns. I share my story to show you that we all come from somewhere, and sometimes it's not good.

We were all born with baggage, and we carry it with us until we figure out how and when to unpack it to lighten our load. Our first piece of luggage is typically our childhood.

Some of us were born into two-parent households, some weren't. Some of us never knew our mothers or fathers. Some of us were raised by grandparents or extended family. Some of us have been homeless or in foster care. The adults who brought us into this world were our first influences and examples of how to live. Whether they sat us down and taught us anything, or just showed up and allowed how they lived to be the example, what we learned—or didn't learn—started right there.

You made decisions, good or bad, based on what you saw. Your environment set your expectations. And that is okay.

You may remember that I started this book talking about forgiveness. Many of us are still harboring resentment towards our parents and the people who raised us for not giving us the great starts that we deserved. That is a piece of baggage that you need to let go of. Forgive them. Free them so you can free yourself.

Our parents and the people who raised us gave us what they had to give. It was impossible for them to teach you what they didn't know. If all they knew was to get a job, put some kind of roof over your head, clothes on your back, and food in your mouth, then that's the blueprint they had to give you. If they lived a life on welfare, then that's what they had to teach you. If all they could do was help you to simply survive in this world, by any means necessary, then that is what they could pass on to you.

Have you ever asked yourself, "How was I supposed to know?"

If no one taught you how to save and spend money wisely, how were you supposed to know? If no one showed you the importance of having a home, how were you supposed to know?

If you didn't have an example of a loving marriage or supportive parents, how were you supposed to know?

Sometimes we naturally learn to navigate life and pick up the things that we didn't know. But if that's not your story, it's okay. You've made a few mistakes trying to figure it out.

But now here comes the kick in the –

We can't stay stuck in the excuse of what we don't know forever.

Once the light is turned on, once our eyes have been opened to new possibilities, what we don't know, what we never got, and even what we don't have, are no longer valid reasons for us to live mediocre lives. Whatever your circumstances are and your challenges have been, at any point, now's your time to put that behind you and learn a new way of living. You've decided that you want a different kind of life. So now what?

It's time to do better. For us. For our communities. For our children.

Beyond achieving financial stability and success for myself, I knew that I wanted a different life for my children than what I had. Before I had them, and even after my firstborn arrived, I had little money, but I had a lot of courage. A lot of belief in myself. And a lot of desire to give my children more than I ever had. Yes, I wanted to give them toys and clothes and watch their faces light up on Christmas morning when they found piles of gifts under the tree. But first, I wanted to give them the security that could only come from a mom and dad who would love them no matter what. I wanted them to have a place they could always call home, and come back to when life got rough. A space where they could dream, play, mess up, and learn from their mistakes, and access to information about better education and building wealth so they could learn from *my* mistakes. All of that came before the fun vacations, new sneakers, and presents.

When we do better, we break the cycle.

THE CURSE OF POVERTY

Some families hand their children success on a silver spoon—while ours handed us generations of struggle, scarcity, and survival.

Debt, poor credit scores, and bad money management are all things that we have been exposed to. We've been surrounded by struggle all our lives. And it began long before we were born, and in some cases, before our parents were born. The curse of poverty has made lack a legacy for many of our families.

As a real estate broker, my agents and I get to help people find their first homes and create a roadmap to ownership. Our clients are often working-class men and women who sometimes thought it was impossible but have a dream of owning a home, and we do everything we can to make that happen for them.

When we sit down and look at their financials for the first time, we don't just see seven years of bad credit and low checking and savings balances. We see the hopes and possibilities of what could be with the right coaching and encouragement. When they understand their options and opportunities, nothing can stop them. Lives are changed, legacies are created, and communities are shifted. If everyone could just see what we see, together we can change the world.

Even if you didn't feel the weight of that struggle, and you grew up with parents and a family who had more than enough, you may still be buying your way into a hole.

When we earn a good salary, but we find ourselves overspending to keep up appearances and a luxury lifestyle, that can be just as detrimental as not making enough money at all. That is still brokenness and a sure-fire way to end up overwhelmed, overextended, and if you're like me, facing the decision to either throw yourself at the mercy of a bankruptcy court or working to pay off debt until you die. Now, I am not judging you. I love nice "things" and the ability to buy whatever I want for myself and my family. But poverty can hide well in Prada. And if you are buying all liabilities and no assets you will always struggle.

Breaking the curse and cycle of poverty in our families requires us to be the first to make better decisions that lead to a better life.

What you can do…

- ❖ **Choose Differently.** This is where the decision comes in. If you want more, then you have to commit to whatever it takes to have it. Make the hard choices.
- ❖ **Start Now.** It's never too late to get it right. Start where you are. Invest in financial knowledge. Budget. Save. Pay down debt. Invest. Give.
- ❖ **Teach Our Children.** Once we create a new path for ourselves, it doesn't stop there. We need to show our children the way. You may not have children of your own, but maybe you have nieces and nephews, godchildren, and cousins. Be the example. And also talk to them about savings and not buying more than they can afford. Teach them the principles of investing, tithing, and giving back to their community.

CHAPTER TWO
BREAKING NEGATIVITY

"Speaking life into a child will open up a world of possibilities"

When my dad told me that I was going to be the first woman president, I believed him. At four feet tall, that dream didn't feel too far out of my reach. I knew I was smart, and there was nothing that I'd tried that I couldn't do. In my mind, I could do and be anything. If someone gave me a shot, I would take it. That's the way I've always lived my life.

I didn't realize how much my dad's words, and the positive affirmations that my family poured into me, mattered. What I heard seeped down into my spirit and stayed there, like a seed that was planted and just continued to grow.

Even when I failed, I didn't doubt myself for long, and I definitely didn't throw my hands up and give up. I was determined to figure it out. I was determined to get back up. I was determined to win. And as far as the world was concerned, I should have done anything but excel. The odds were stacked against me. I didn't come from money. I am black. I am a woman. I didn't go to college. I've been criticized and counted out. I've been homeless, but never hopeless. And certainly never helpless. All because somebody spoke life into me before I could do it for myself.

I now know how lucky I was to have someone who believed in me and who spoke to the greatness in me. I know people personally who didn't have that. And I've watched how that lack of affirmation and positivity has impacted their lives. They've yet to rise up to their potential. They don't chase dreams or pursue passions. They live limited lives when they could have and be so much more. Their end was defined before they even got a chance to begin. All because no one thought they were important enough to believe in.

THOUGHTS BECOME TRUTHS

The danger about environments where people constantly talk and think negatively is that eventually, they wear you down. And once negative thoughts find a way in, it's not long before they become your truth. Constant negativity will break you. If it already has, you have to put yourself back together.

Maybe someone never told you that you were smart or beautiful or handsome or capable. Or maybe it wasn't what they didn't say that hurt— it was what they did tell you:

"You ain't never going to be nothing."
"You can't do that! You're too (fill in the blank with color, gender, economic status)…"
"Nobody is going to let you…"
These are the types of lies that can scar you for life. But only if you allow it. Find new truths about yourself and your life. You are nothing that they said you were. You can do whatever it is that you decide to do. You don't need permission or approval. There is no one who has to allow you in.

Your new truth is that you are rewriting your history. Defining your success. Deserving more. Teaching yourself. Growing. Reaching. Rising. Take that truth and run with it.

SEE IT SO YOU CAN BELIEVE IT

In high school, I had regular history classes, where black people were barely discussed and celebrated. We could count on learning about slavery, and during Black History Month, a few of our heroes like Harriet Tubman, George Washington Carver, Dr. Martin Luther King, Jr., and Rosa Parks. That was it. Centuries of history and achievement reduced to a few days of the year.

It was almost by accident, by certainly not coincidence, that I started to follow my love for history to books outside of class. When I did, I was floored by what I found. Black history was so much more than slaves and the struggle for civil rights. Much more. We were descendants of royalty. Kings and Queens. Architects. Artisans. Attorneys. Mathematicians, doctors, and scientists. There was Black Wall Street. Self-made millionaires. We owned banks. We created our own self-sufficient communities and economies. Black people weren't poor, broken people. We were significant. We were unlike any other people who had ever walked this earth. Excellence flowed through our veins.

From that point on, my outlook completely changed, about myself and our race as a whole. I started reading everything I could about black history that I could find. Seeing how great we were, how we've always been, lit a fire in me. I didn't just want to be successful for myself, I wanted to help our community to reclaim the success that was rightfully ours. I wanted the world to see us for who and what we were. Regal. Affluent. Mediocracy wasn't an option. I saw something different. And that made me want to be different.

When we shift the lens of our lives, amazing things happen. We begin to realize that there is so much more to us and our lives. We develop an appetite for success. We want to stretch, to go further, faster. We want more.

Looking at your life from a space of limitation and lack is like looking through a filthy, foggy glass and hoping to still make out whatever is on the other side. It's impossible to see clearly. Clean the glass. In fact, bust that mirror up and find a new one. Change everything you see. Start here:

- ❖ **Change Your Space.** Get out of places and away from people with a negative mindset and limited thinking. It's rare that you'll find people who want more for you than they want for themselves. If everyone you know is stuck where they are, you have to shift.

- ❖ **Change Your Soundtrack.** That negative thought loop that is in your head has to go. If you find yourself doubting more than believing, change the channel. Affirm yourself with positive thoughts, all day every day. When you can't find your own voice, turn up the volume on someone else's who believes in you.

- ❖ **Change Your Spirit.** Negativity can get in your soul and permeate not only what you think about yourself, but other people. If don't have anything good to say most of the time, check that critical spirit at the door.

CHAPTER THREE
BREAKING THE BROKE MENTALITY

"Words are singularly the most powerful force available to humanity. We can choose to use this force constructively with words of encouragement, or destructively using words of despair. Words have energy and power with the ability to help, to heal, to hinder, to hurt, to harm, to humiliate and to humble."

~Yehuda Berg

"I'm broke."
We've heard those words more times than we know. We've heard people say it so much, that it's become a part of our everyday language, so normal that we don't even think twice about it. We don't question it. We don't stop to think how we got there, about the series of decisions that led to not having a dime or dollar, enough to pay our bills, or to buy the things we want and need. Especially if the person saying it is staring back at us in the mirror.

We accept being broke for what it is—a way of life. A state of existence that cannot be challenged or changed. We've come to accept that where we are is where we always have to be.

And that it is biggest lie that has ever been told—and we believed it.

We've bought into the lie for so long, that we've forgotten who we really are. That's the thing about believing a lie. It will inevitably become your truth. And that truth begins to guide everything else in your life, without you having to give it a second thought. If you think something long enough, your actions will begin to align accordingly.

It's a subconscious self-sabotage that happens and you don't realize it until the damage has been done. What we think about ourselves, what we can do, and what we can have manifests into how we move.

So we get money, we spend it. We have a home, but we convince ourselves that it's not big enough, so we upgrade. Our cars are paid off and running well enough to get us from Point A to Point B, but we tell ourselves that it's time for a new model. We get an unexpected blessing of extra cash, and instead of paying off a debt, paying a few months ahead on a utility or some other recurring bill, investing in a few shares of stock or a CD, or just letting the money sit in a savings account and accrue interest, we find something to buy, something to eat, somewhere to go. Why? Because looking at a zero balance is so normal that to think of the possibility of anything else doesn't seem sustainable or real. That is what a broke mentality will create in your life. A broke mentality will push us to buy things we can't afford. To not invest in assets that grow wealth. To always be consumers instead of creators. Broke is the shackle keeping us enslaved to poverty and mediocrity. A broke mentality is bondage.

A broke mentality is how you can earn over $200,000 a year, and find yourself standing in line for assistance to get your utilities turned back on and contemplating food stamps. Or to be in position to purchase and renovate a building or a block of homes, but choose to blow money on cars and a lavish lifestyle. A broke mentality is how you put all your blood, sweat, and tears into building a business and life for yourself and your family, only to have it all taken away. A broke mentality is how you can fight your way out of the poverty that plagued you as a child and cursed your entire family, but look your children in the face and repeat the same mistakes.

That was me. And I am here today so that it doesn't have to be you, too.

If I've learned nothing else, I know that broke is in the mind of the beholder. It starts with what you think of yourself and how you act. And being broke comes from being broken.

We've talked about what breaks us in life, how we got here. It's what we've been taught and shown about money and a quality of life. Where and how we lived as children and how those habits followed us into adulthood. The lack of positive affirmation and the negative perspective that people in our lives have had of us that formed how we think about and see ourselves. Even in church, we're told that we receive blessings *in spite* of our brokenness. That we're not worthy, but that God gives it to us anyway. But I want to challenge that. I know, it's bold. But hear me. That message is filtered through someone else's interpretation of who you are and what you deserve. Someone who has been conditioned to believe that scraps and not surplus is all that we are ever entitled to. Their beliefs have become yours. All of that has played a part in reshaping our thinking and defining who we are. What you think *is*.

The truth is that God wants you to have everything that you desire. All that He asks is that you be a good steward over what He does give. You don't have to prove and pray your way to acceptance and worthiness with Him. He already knows who and what you are, and what you deserve. He created you. You just need to accept it as your truth and act accordingly.

When I talk about being better with your money and the blessings that God has given you, I don't want you to adopt a spirit of scarcity. I am here to empower and encourage, not to discourage you from having what you desire, regardless of what that is. Abundance is and should be yours. But I do want you to begin to think, and act, differently. I want you to see your spending habits, how you earn and manage money, from a different perspective.

I want you to sow the seeds and grow a harvest before you spend.

I want you to be able to buy what you want with ease, and not with a sense of the guilt, fear, and shame that comes when you impulsively buy something you want, and regret it later when you need money but don't have it.

I want you to hold your head up and take pride in what you have, instead of being embarrassed or humiliated when you have to walk into a bank for a loan and lay out your financial history before a stranger who will judge you for making bad decisions.

I want you to think, act, and speak from a place of surplus and not shortage.

You've been told all of your life that you can't have and you can't do. But today we will speak seeds of wealth and plant them in the sweet soil of belief. Then we'll watch them grow.

YOU ARE WHAT YOU SAY YOU ARE

When you say things like, "I'm broke" you're telling the universe to keep you in the state of lack and you're programming your mind to keep you there. Your words are powerful and prophetic, and what you say becomes real. If you want to have more, you have to speak it into existence. You have to shift your language.

You are no longer broke. In the words of Iyanla Vanzant, "You are not broke. You are temporarily out of cash." That is how you redirect your words to completely change the results that you call forth into your life.

You may not have a lot, or any, money in your pocket or purse right now. But in your mind, you are rich. In your hands, you're holding skills and the ability to do something, to create something, to apply something, that will shift your situation. You are whole and complete, regardless of how low your balance is. The cents in your checking account, don't determine your sense of self-worth. Dollars don't define who you are. You cannot spend your way into self-esteem. But you can speak.

To own your words, you have to remember who you are.

You were born brilliant, bold, and beautiful. Your ancestors are the most powerful people who ever lived. The beauty and the blessing of being who you are, coming from where you come from, is that you are capable. You are purpose personified, created in the image and likeness of God. You have an eternal access to abundance, wherever you are, because you an Heir of a King. I want you to hear that, to get that, to let that sink in and sit in your soul and your spirit. I know we sit in church and hear words like that all the time. But we don't believe it. We believe it for the pastor and the First Lady, but not for ourselves. We don't believe it because we don't see the fruit of abundance and affluence in our lives.

But have you realized that you haven't reached up and grabbed your fruit from the tree?

If you did that, and looked down at your hands, you would see what's there. You are resourceful. You are resilient, and that just hasn't built you to be beaten down for the rest of your life—it's built you to bounce back. And when you do, you

come back to be better than before, and not back to shrinking, struggle, and status quo.
You have more. You make more. You gather more.
You do more. You build more. You create more.
You ARE more.
Affirm it.
Speak things as though they already are.

THE POWER OF GRATEFUL PRAYER

Speaking abundance into your life is one of the most important things that you can do. You can read and absorb information and inspiration, but the truth power is on your tongue. When you speak something, it activates. And the more you say it, the more real it becomes. You begin to change how you feel, how you move, and how you see everything around you. Your back becomes straighter. Your mind becomes clearer. You start to expect grace, goodness, and greatness to come, in every way. And so it does. Years ago, I began thanking God for things that I wanted, as if He'd already given them to me. I thank Him for peace of mind. I thank Him for flow in my finances. I thank Him for my husband and children being successful in whatever they do. As I saw the results of this things manifesting in my life, my courage increased. I became bolder. I thank God for an office full of productive agents. I thank Him for millions of dollars in gross sales for our team. I thank Him for allowing me to inspire greatness in my team and everyone I meet, to travel and speak more so I can help more people to change their lives.

I don't stop there. Here are some things that I am currently thanking God for every day:

- "Thank you, God, for my healthy, happy, and strong family."
- "Thank you, God, for my strong marriage."
- "Thank you, God, for my new business opportunity that will yield me xx this year."
- "Thank you, God, for my 20-pound weight loss."
- "Thank you, God, for my Ted Talk."

Now that you have an idea of what I am thanking God for and fully expecting to receive, I want you to put this to work for yourself. Before we go on, take a moment to think about some things that you are thanking God for that you believe will happen. Write them down here.

_____

_____

_____

_____

_____

_____

If you are stuck on where to start, here are some prayers of gratitude to start activating power in your life:

- "Thank you, God, that I am enough."
- "Thank you, God, that I will have freedom."
- "Thank you, God, that I am able to help my family."
- "Thank you, God, that I can do everything that's in my heart to do."
- "Thank you, God, that I can do all things."

For the next 21 days, I want you to commit to creating some new habits to create space to thank God, prime your mind for positivity, and begin speaking abundance and overflow over your life:

- ❖ **Meditate in the mornings.** Meditation is a peaceful and powerful way to connect with God. Start with five minutes a day and work your way up to more. Get into a quiet space and clear your mind. And just sit back and allow God to pour into you. Let the peace come. Let the understanding come. Let the answers and the ideas come.

❖ **Wake up with a grateful heart.** Your house may not be what you want it to be, but thank Him for it anyway. Your car may not be the newest model, and you may be holding your breath every time you turn the key, but it started, so thank Him. Your kids may be acting up and those grades aren't where they need to be, but thank Him for the blessing to be a mother anyway.

❖ **Say it out loud.** We have a tendency to want to pray in silence. But you don't have anything to hide, so your words to God don't have to be in secret. Let them come out of your mouth and fall on your own ears. It doesn't matter where you are. Say it.

❖ **Commit to it.** Like brushing your teeth and getting dressed, your power prayers have to become a part of your daily life. I set an alarm on my phone for 6:00 a.m. and again for 8:00 p.m. every day to remind myself to stop whatever I am doing to say my affirmations. Choose the times that work for you, but be sure to set a specific time to do this every day.

BREAKING THE B.R.O.K.E. CODE WITH AFFIRMATIONS
TO CHANGE YOUR LIFE

Now let's go back to The B.R.O.K.E. Code, and see how we can turn affirmation into the actions that will change you, your situation, and your life forever.

What I know to be true is being broke is in the mind of the beholder. It starts with what you think of yourself, how you act. The state of your life is a direct interpretation of your thoughts. When you say things like "I'm broke" you're telling the universe to keep you in the state of lack and you're programming your mind to keep you there.

"Words are singularly the most powerful force available to humanity. We can choose to use this force constructively with words of encouragement, or destructively using words of despair. Words have energy and power with the ability to help, to heal, to hinder, to hurt, to harm, to humiliate and to humble." —Yehuda Berg

Broke is the shackle keeping you enslaved to poverty and mediocrity. Here's how you break free from Broke Bondage.

I've created a specific set of affirmations to help you to activate the power of shifting your life in a new direction, and taking specific steps towards what you want.

Belief

I don't mean just believing in God, or even just believing in yourself. I mean believing that you deserve everything life and God has for you. Many of us say that we are believers, we are faithful, and that we trust God, but when it comes to wanting something big for ourselves, when it comes down to it, we don't really believe we can have it. In fact, if we're honest, we don't actually believe we *should* have it. But you should have abundance. You should have access to everything that God has and created, because He is your Father, too.

You have to truly believe that you don't have to live in lack and scarcity, but that you deserve happiness and freedom, both mentally and financially. Success is not for a small segment of the population. It's for you. The walk towards anything that you desire begins with believing it can happen. The first step to breaking the code is having the BELIEF that you deserve it!

Say these affirmations daily or choose your own and write them below:

I deserve to win.

I deserve to be successful.

I deserve happiness.
I deserve abundance.

_____

_____

_____

_____

_____

_____

<u>Ready</u>

You have to be ready for opportunities. Being ready means, you are prepared and made plans. It means you've already visualized in your mind, wrote it, spoke it, and took action on it, now you're READY to receive it. You are in position. You're only able to take on new opportunities when you are ready to receive them.

Being ready isn't just accepting whatever comes your way. Readiness is being open and available for your destiny. So you are not settling for anything that is not in line with the direction that God has for your life.

Say these affirmations daily or choose your own and write them below:

I am ready to receive.

I will stay ready, so I don't have to get ready.

I am ready to take on the world.

I am ready to take a risk.

_____

_____

_____

_____

_____

_____

<u>O</u>bsessed

In the book, *Think and Grow Rich*, Napoleon Hill studied 500 millionaires. All of them were chasing different dreams and achieving in different ways, but the one common thread they all shared was they were obsessed with their success. You will only succeed when whatever it is you decide to do becomes your obsession. The average person just wishes or hopes for a promotion, a raise, or recognition. But a high achiever is obsessed with obtaining those things. Obsession will push you to train for the marathon when your legs can hardly move. Obsession will get you out of bed two hours early to study for the license. Obsession will put every extra penny towards that credit card or leave work at 5:00 p.m. every evening to get home to your kids, regardless of who else needs something from you in the office that can wait.

When a burning desire is mixed with strong willpower, it produces enough fuel to carry you to greatness. Get obsessed with your goals.

Say these affirmations daily or choose your own and write them below:

I am obsessed with success.

I am obsessed with my life.

I am obsessed with making a difference.

I am obsessed with helping others.

I am obsessed with leaving a legacy.

_____

_____

_____

_____

_____

_____

Knowledgeable

The average person may read a book or two. Maybe even a couple of magazines per year. The average CEO reads voraciously to elevate their learning and self-development. The only thing that separates an average person from a CEO is not the fact that they are smarter, it is that they invest in themselves. They know their value. They know they are their biggest investment and commodity.

After mindset, a lack education and information is the next reason why we're stuck in our brokenness. Many of us have not because we know not. Once we're clear on what we want to do, then our next step is to fill ourselves with as much knowledge on that particular thing as we can find. Google is your best friend—anything that you need to find can start there. Seek out people who have already done what you are trying to do successfully. Ask someone who knows more about it than you do. Read something written by someone who knows more than you. Get obsessed with learning. Get into rooms with people who can help you grow, elevate, and expand.

Because I have a PHD (A Public High-School Diploma), I HAVE to continue to educate myself in a variety of different ways. Whether it's getting training or going to seminars, workshops, or conferences, I am constantly feeding myself to close the gap between what I know and what I don't. I don't have formal training, and I've got a chip on my shoulder because of it. So in order to chip away at the chip, I constantly have to fill my mind with knowledge to build, grow, and sustain. You will never catch me unprepared or coming to any table without knowing everything I need to know to understand what I am walking in to.

Adopt that same philosophy in your own life. Devour knowledge that will lead you to your destiny.

Say these affirmations daily or choose your own and write them below:

I will read _____ books per month.

I will network _____ times per month.

I will go to _____ trainings per month.

I will utilize my resources to learn all I can about my goal.

_____

_____

_____

_____

_____

_____

<u>E</u>conomical

Being economical means that you are wise about wealth. Approach opportunities sensibly and make wise investments. If you want to break The Code, you have to exercise restraint at times. You have to be willing to sacrifice. Now may not be the time to buy the bigger house, the new car, or take the trip. The things you want to do right now, you may not be able to do them. Let go of the "right now" mindset, and embrace patience. Grow your seed, and I promise you that all the things you can't have now will come with ease later. Discipline will accelerate your abundance and growth. When you are able to sow more, you will reap more. Work, wait, and watch. You'll see what I mean.

Sacrifice will apply to every area of your life, and to any dream you desire to pursue. Whether it's time or money, you will be required to give up things at times. If you want to be an entrepreneur, you'll have to give up that 9-to-5 mindset. As you're growing your business, there will be sleepless nights, growing pains, and at times feast or famine. Now is the time to practice separating yourself from that paycheck-to-paycheck, coffee-to-clock-out mentality. When you work for yourself, there will be times when the checks are few and far between, and the calls from clients don't stop when the sun sets.

Prepare for the success you want now. You don't have money or time to squander and waste.

You have legacies to build.

Say these affirmations daily or choose your own and write them below:

I will sacrifice now so it will be greater later.

I will make wise financial decisions.

I will maintain excellent credit.

I will live beneath my means.

_____

_____

_____

_____

_____

_____

CHAPTER FOUR
BREAKING THE F.E.A.R.

"How would you feel if you knew you needed FEAR to succeed?"

Fear is one of those things that will hold you back without you even realizing it. It's sneaky. And it comes in so many forms.

There are the fears that feel familiar. Fear (as in reverence) of God. Fear of bad things that have happened to other people and could happen to us, as in False Evidence Appearing Real. Fear of success. The list goes on and on.

But when you are fighting for success, facing obstacles that seem too tall to climb, and bringing a dream to fruition that nobody may see possibility in but you, there is a different type of fear that comes up. It's a kind of FEAR that many high achievers have experienced on their journey to greatness. It's the real F.E.A.R. that you'll have to break to get to your destiny, and this is what it looks like:

- **F**ailure
- **E**mbarrassment
- **A**ll In
- **R**isk

Let's break it down.

Failure

I have failed more times than I can count. From job losses to bankruptcy, failure was, and still is, my fuel. When each of those things happened, I refused to let them stop me. I could not let the potential of failure detour me from reaching my goals. It was the failed attempts, lessons learned, and sheer determination that catapulted me to the next level.

During my bankruptcy proceeding, I walked into that courthouse as if the weight of the world was on my shoulders. I carried so much guilt and shame along with that debt. It was hard enough to have to face your spouse and immediate family when something like that happens. But it's a whole different situation when you wonder if neighbors and colleagues, hell, anybody, notices that you aren't driving the expensive cars or that investment property you had went into foreclosure. Going to court was like airing out my dirty laundry on a larger scale. I felt exposed for the world to see. At that point, that was the biggest failure of my life.

Going before the judge and being granted the permission to proceed with my filing was one of the best things that ever happened to me. I had shed too many tears and carried too much stress, and I knew I needed to let it all go and start over.

I went into that courtroom expecting that the judgment would be in my favor, and it was. Although I had to give up my Mercedes and some of my properties, I also gave up all my debt in exchange for my piece of mind. Yes, bankruptcy was a huge setback, but it was an absolute necessity to position me for my comeback. Bankruptcy was indeed a failure. Mismanaging my money was a failure. But had I not gone through that, I wouldn't have been equipped to walk fully in what I believe to be God's purpose for my life, which is leading my community to financial freedom and showing them the path to break free from the bondage of struggle—starting with their pockets. It was all part of God's bigger plan for my life. Even if I deviated from my road to success with a mistake, God would not strip everything He ever had for me because I made some bad choices. He let me fail so I could fly. And I am more than okay with that. I meet people all the time who have filed bankruptcy more than two decades ago, and they've been paralyzed ever since. They are afraid to buy new homes or do anything involving credit. They refuse to move forward, to do more, live better, or be more as a result of that one misstep. It is a business decision that millions of people make every day. It isn't a stigma or a scarlet letter that you need to wear on your chest. Take the hit, learn the lesson, and move on.

You may not need to file bankruptcy, but on this road to success, failure is imminent. The business idea may not pan out the first time around. The first time you ask for the promotion, you may be told no. Plans fall through and dreams take detours. You may fall flat on your pretty face and that's okay. Failing is inevitable and essential to your growth. Like a basic training preparing you for war, failing is just a part of the process. So don't run from it. Run to it. And always remember—it's not how you fall. It's how you get back up.

Face Your Failures

What are some failures you've had in your life?

_____

_____

_____

_____

_____

How did you deal with those failures?

_____

_____

_____

_____

_____

_____

What do you wish you would've done
differently?

_____

_____

_____

_____

_____

How are you better because of them?

_____

_____

_____

_____

_____

_____

_Use these affirmations to help you shift your
mindset about failure. Say these affirmations daily
or choose your own and write them below:_
Failure is not an option.
I will not let the FEAR of failure stop me.
Can't is not in my vocabulary.
I can do all things.

_____

_____

_____

_____

_____

Embarrassment

When I first started in real estate, I had no money. Most of the time I was living on prayer and a gas tank stuck on "E." But I was determined to make my dreams happened. Whenever I took a client to see a home, I'd be praying three prayers, hard:

1. That they'd overlook the fact that I was not driving a luxury car like my colleagues;

2. They would like me enough to call me back after the first showing;

3. They would be willing to write an offer so that I could finally make a commission.

There were many months that I spent with people who didn't buy for one reason or another and wasted my time. I chalked it up as a learning experience.

In June of my first year, I lucked out and my next-door neighbor allowed me to list her home. Through that listing, I picked up a couple of good buyers, two couples that were in the market and ready to buy. One of them made it easy for me to hide the ripped-up interior of my old car by following behind me, which is actual agent/client protocol. And then there was Linda and Tom. Linda and Tom were an older couple who had sold their home in the Bay Area and were looking to downsize in Stockton. I met them one day to talk about possibilities and show them a few properties. But instead of going to their car to follow me as I asked, Linda and Tom walked right over to my raggedy Ford Windstar minivan and hopped right on in. I was so nervous and embarrassed. The seats and floors were stained, and I knew there was a strong possibility that it could stall at any time and an even greater possibility the back door could fly open as well. With Linda in the front and Tom in the back, I drove carefully but my heart was beating out of my chest. I avoided every bump and every pothole to try to keep the car running and that darn door closed. I was successful with one of the two. As I chatted with Linda, I turned the corner and looked in the rearview mirror. My eyes got big as saucers as the door flew open and I saw Tom holding on for dear life as he struggled to stay in and close it.

I was so mortified that I could have slid right under the driver's seat—and stayed there. FOREVER!

Here I am already struggling with my own thoughts, fears, and insecurities. I was young, black, a woman, not well dressed, and driving raggedy cars. Some people might have given up, but I used that embarrassment and those shortcomings as an incentive, and I proceeded to provide the best care and customer service. I was going to be the best, most knowledgeable, most loyal, greatest service giving agent that they had ever experienced to work with. They were going to forget about all what I didn't have and focus on my qualities. Sure enough, I won them over. We found them a beautiful home and the day I gave them their keys, Linda told me, "Constance, no matter what you do, no matter how big you get in this business (because I know you will), please don't ever change." I have and will remember those words always. That experience kept me both humble and hungry.

At times on your journey, you may look foolish. You probably will have something happen to you that could make the average person hang their head and hide.

Your raggedy car might stop running.

Somebody will publically bash your business.

You'll lose an office space because you can't afford to pay the rent.

You will get fired from a job in the middle of the work day while your co-workers whisper about what happened.

You may come home and find the utility company putting that bright envelope in your screen door; or better yet, the bank putting your stuff on the curb.

Your kid will get suspended from school and you'll feel like the worst mother on the planet.

The love of your life may decide you are not the love of theirs and leave.

Any of these things may come with the pursuit of success, and the life that always happens in between. If you aren't willing to be laughed at, to be talked about, to be humiliated for the world to see, to face people who will say, "I told you that wouldn't work!" or "I knew you couldn't do it anyway," to take three steps back as soon as you take two steps forward, then you don't want it badly enough.

Are you willing to be uncomfortable? Are you willing to be laughed at and talked about? Are you willing to let the world see you with your pants down?

If the answer is yes, then you're ready to move.

Move Past the Embarrassment

Describe a moment in your journey when you've been embarrassed.

_____

_____

_____

_____

_____

What are some insecurities in your life that have stopped you from reaching your goals?

_____

_____

_____

_____

_____

How will you push through the insecurities to reach your goals?

_____

_____

_____

_____

_____

Fill in the following declarations.

_____ will no longer be a hindrance in my success.

I will not let _____ stop me from reaching my goals.

I will push past my fear of _____ to reach my goal.

Use these affirmations to help you shift your mindset about embarrassment. Say these affirmations daily or choose your own and write them below:

I have everything I need to be successful.
Nothing can stop me.
I am comfortable in being uncomfortable.

_____

_____

_____

_____

_____

All In

Getting laid off from my corporate job saved my life. Had they not let me go, I wouldn't have been forced to pursue my real estate dreams full on. I could have easily gotten stuck there, and comfortable in the security of retirement, benefits, and direct deposit. Oh, and I forgot to mention one more thing that could have started to feel real good—mediocrity. No, not me.

My husband and I started mapping out our money months before my last day. The plan was to use my severance and unemployment for our small, miscellaneous bills and my business expenses, and in turn, my husband would take care of the mortgage and everything else. He was totally supportive of my dreams and encouraged me to do whatever I needed to do, knowing that it wasn't just about me—it was about us.

I remember driving home on my last day. It was bittersweet. The security blanket was now gone but still, I was excited like I had never been before. I couldn't help but think of all the possibilities that lay ahead for us. That two-hour ride home was filled with smiles and giggles; it felt like I got home in half the time. I floated through the door excited and ready to take on the world, only to see a strange look on my husband's face. A look that definitely couldn't have meant anything good.

"I got fired," he blurted out.

That was the day that our Plan B went out the window. And there was no way that I was going back to a job that meant that I'd be two hours away from my baby girl, and living to work instead of working to live. So that became the day that we decided to go all in.

My husband immediately got a job paying a little more than minimum wage to pay as many bills as he could, and our plan was to use my three-month severance to cover our mortgage. The hope was that by the time I obtained my real estate license, I could hit the ground running and the commission would kick in right as our savings ran out. If all went according to plan, it would take 30 days for me to start bringing money in. I didn't sell my first house until six months later.

That was six months of focusing on nothing else but working my business. I studied sales and marketing. I cold called. I knocked on doors. I drove clients from house to house, spending the last few dollars in my pocket on a few gallons of gas at time since I could rarely afford to fill up. I still have the spreadsheet I created the first year and use it to this day to track my bills. Every month in that spreadsheet, you see no money coming in, but money was being paid out to cover my bills and my business expenses. It was a struggle.

Yes, there were days I got discouraged. Yes, there were times I wanted to give up, but there were no Plan Bs. This absolutely had to work. There was no other option. There was no other way. And that commitment, that willingness to go all in, eventually paid off. Had I continued working in Corporate America, making $70k per year, it would have taken me over 80 years to make what I have been able to make in this business. More importantly, the experiences I've been able to create and the people I've been able to help as a result are just as valuable as any amount of money I've made along the way.

Throw that Plan B out of the window. It may be a job. It may be a savings account that you know you have no business touching, so you need to live way below your means so you don't have to. It may be refusing to stop showing up to speak to crowds even though, right now, the room is empty.

Going all in is about you betting on you because YOU are your greatest commodity.

Put your plan together. Sacrifice and work the plan. The plan may get interrupted. You may have slight detours but stay the course. Reaping and sowing are universal principles. "Don't get weary in well doing, for in due season, you will reap your harvest" (Galatians 6:9).

Keep going.

Put Your ALL IN to the Test
How have you gone ALL IN for your dreams?

_____

_____

_____

_____

_____

If you haven't gone ALL IN yet, what are some things you can do differently?

_____

_____

_____

_____

_____

If you don't have the ability to dedicate 100% to your dream, how can you change that?

_____

_____

_____

_____

_____

Use these affirmations to help you find the determination, strength, and focus to go all in for your dreams. Say these affirmations daily or choose your own and write them below:
I'm going ALL IN.
I'm a sure thing.
I am my biggest investment.
There is no Plan B.

_____

_____

_____

_____

_____

Risk

There are three things that you can count on:

1. Failure and risk go hand in hand.

2. With no risk, there are no rewards.

3. Where there is risk, there is no regret.

When you think back over your life, do you only want memories of what you didn't do? Do you want a life full of "What ifs" or "Should haves"? Or, when it's all said and done, do you want to be able to say you tried—you did it—even if you failed?

I could throw a book of clichés at you, and tell you everything that you are missing out on when you don't take chances. But I know you've probably heard them all before. You've heard the success stories of all the people who put everything they had on the line for a dream, and, in the end, they won—big. You know what's at stake when you play small in this life and refuse to bet on everything but yourself. You know that nothing worth having in this life will come to you inside of spaces that are familiar and comfortable. Success requires you to stretch. So the question is, if you know all this, and you've read everything that I've shared with you so far in this book, can you honestly walk away comfortable with where you are?

If I can push you to do one thing, it would be to take a chance on at least one dream that you've been sitting on.

I've put it all on the line more than once in my life and career, and the rewards have far outweighed the failures and the uncertainty of the risk. In fact, hesitation to take risk has cost me. When I opened my real estate brokerage, I actually started a year later than I was supposed to. I was scared and playing small. Taking on my own company and all the responsibilities that came with it made me nervous. Staying an independent agent was safer. I finally decided to go for it, and while I've been successful, I may have been a lot further than I am now.

I never forgot that lesson, so when opportunity knocks today, I run to the door. When marijuana was legalized in California, it piqued my interest, but I knew nothing about it. I met a gentleman at a conference, and we had a conversation about the benefits of investing in the marijuana business. One of the things that stuck out most to me was the hundreds of thousands of black men that were doing time in prison due to selling marijuana and now white men are making millions of dollars in the same industry. If we don't have a seat at the table, we risk being on the menu.

When I returned home, I began to study voraciously about the topic. I bought marijuana stock and looked at different investment options for any opportunity that would come my way. One day, I got a call from a girlfriend about an investment opportunity in a dispensary. My only question was how much of a check do I need to write. It was a six-figure investment. Of course, I didn't write the check without doing my due diligence, but that's how serious I was about the opportunity. I met with the organization and they gave me a very conservative prospectus, but I had done my research and knew the potential was much higher than they were estimating it to be. They outlined the risk; however, I understood and was most interested in the reward. I wrote the check.

Due to regulations, things didn't go according to plan, some investors pulled out, the city caused delays, but the dispensary finally opened ten months after their original planned date. Some of my friends who knew I made the investment questioned it. "Is this real? Is this going to happen? Did they take your money?" Trust me, I fully vetted the opportunity, and one thing I know is I'm not willing to risk what I'm not willing to lose. Had I not made a dime, I was at peace. However, the dispensary is now open, profitable, and grossing nearly one million dollars a month. The risk that I took on this investment is now a college fund for my children, retirement for myself, and legacy money for future generations.

I am considered a high-risk investor. Sometimes I have great returns and other times I have losses. But ultimately, I have a plan and a goal and that's to provide a certain lifestyle for my family, maintain a successful business, and to help others to create the life of their dreams. I can only do that if I stretch myself, get uncomfortable, and take risks.

Imagine yourself standing on a ledge, afraid to jump because you are afraid to fall. But what if you jump and instead of falling, you fly?

Are you ready to test your wings?

You have to risk it all to have it all.

CHAPTER FIVE
BREAKING INTO YOUR PURPOSE

"The two most important days in your life are the day you are born and the day you find out why."
~Mark Twain

There are some questions in this life that only God can answer. You won't find them in a book. The wisest woman in your life can't give it to you. You can ask every person you meet, attend every conference, hire every coach, and you still will not find what you're looking for. That's because while those people and those places will position you to receive confirmation, you first need to have a conversation. That conversation will tell you exactly what you need to know. It will give you the answer that you've been searching for and seeking. But, first, you have to ask the question:

"What was I put on this Earth for?"

His answer is your purpose, the assignment that God has only given you to complete. His answer is the reason why you wake up every morning, why you are restless, and obsessed, and willing to put it all on the line. His answer is why you were born. His answer is your guide for every move that you'll make from this point forward. Don't rest until you have your answer.

My guess is that there have been some signs around you. There have been some spaces that have made you know you belong in. There have been problems that you see clear solutions to, when no one else does. There are people that you have talked to that you know were destined to meet you, so you could help them in some way. There have been things that you've done, things that you've lived through, things that connect the dots of your destiny that have happened in your life. Those are all God's way of revealing your purpose to you.

But you're still unsure. He's waiting for you to ask for your answer to give the confirmation, the certainty, that you've been looking for.

Ask Him so you can finally break into what you are called to do.

When I look over the landscape of my life now, the signs that pointed to my purpose have always been there. My family's financial struggles. My father's pride in owning his own home, even when he had little else. Being homeless. The discomfort of my own struggles to build a business, to purchase my own property, and to lose everything I had. Through all of that, I never lost the belief that I was on the purposeful path that God placed me on. Times have been hard, really hard, but once I started moving, there was always something down on the inside of me that told me to keep going. To keep trying. To keep serving and the reward would come. With purpose comes provision. There is elevation and abundance attached to your assignment. So, if you feel that urge to go bigger, MOVE!

Four years after being licensed as a real estate salesperson, I passed the Broker exam and became a Broker Associate of another large real estate firm. I had no desire to open my own business, it was just something else to add to professional achievements. Being a black woman with no post-secondary education, I knew I had to run faster, jump higher, and work harder than my counterparts. I needed that extra somethin', somethin' to rock with the best.

I always thought I'd have to work for a big, established company to be successful, and for a while, I was. I consistently ranked in top 5 and top 10 in a company of over 500 agents, most of them white men. But there was something in me that nudged me to step out on my own. I heard it, I felt it, but my fears even talked me into taking a management position at that brokerage for a while, rather than move. More money. But I was sacrificing all that was out there for me and the people who I needed to help.

In 2009, God placed very heavily on my heart that it was time to leave my comfort zone and open my own business. From the very beginning, I'd done business differently. While most companies teach you that real estate is all about the transaction, I never felt that way. I believed that selling homes was about transformation. I wondered how many lives I could change as a result of helping one person become a homeowner. How will this help their immediate family, extended family and build their legacy? How can I help them create a wealth plan and expand their wealth portfolio by teaching them how to build their wealth through their credit and use their credit as leverage?

I knew that part of God's purpose for my life was to open a real estate company that enabled me and others to help people in a very special way.

I Googled absolutely everything. I created my business plan, my corporation, the processes, procedures, and the infrastructure. This took nearly a year of development. Then, I was ready to look for an office.

As I started searching with my assistant, Glenda, we were led to a space with five private offices. I was thinking it would only be the two of us and maybe one other person to start off, but Glenda was adamant that we'd found our home. I was terrified to make that large of a commitment, but she challenged me right out of my fears, reminding me that I wasn't starting out as small as I thought. She knew that all the agents at the brokerage that I managed were willing to leave with me. And she was right. When we opened the doors to Catalyst Real Estate Professionals on July 1, 2010, every one of those five offices were filled. We were a powerful team. Eight women. Two Hispanic, two Filipina, one White, and three African-American. I wanted a group of women who were as diverse as the population we serve so that people could see themselves in every one of us, whether they were buying a home or seeking examples of what success looked like in their own backyard. Even the name of the company speaks to who we are. By definition, Catalyst means "an agent that speeds significant change." That is who we are. We're change agents. We're rapidly accelerating abundance and wealth for people in our community.

A lifetime of preparation, one year of focus and laying the foundation, and on day one, we were fully operational and opened for business. In our first year, we closed enough transactions to rank us in the top 10 companies in Stockton. Since then, we've grown to become the largest African-American-owned real estate firm in Northern

California. We've expanded our offerings to become a direct lender, which means we can lend our own money, and we're also offering unique benefits such as revenue sharing where we invest in our agents' personal wealth.

All of this happened once I broke into my purpose. I broke the cycle of poverty for my family, and for so many others. I broke negativity. I broke fear. I broke barriers. I broke rules that said black women can't be successful, or that minorities can never become independently wealthy though entrepreneurship.

I asked God for the answer. He spoke and I listened.

Dig deep into your heart, mind, and spirit. Ask the one question that will change your life: "What was I put on this Earth for?"

It may not be revealed in one sitting. You may have to keep asking. Sit and just reflect. Wait on an answer for the clear vision for your life.

You have a purpose that you have been designed for. You have a specific assignment that only you can do. There may be other people who are called to solve the same problem as you. But there is something unique about how you do it. There are hundreds of thousands of real estate brokerages across the country. But I believe that every client that comes into our office was sent to us to help them in a way that only we can. We are champions for people who believed that their present circumstances and challenges counted them out. That having a landlord was their destiny. We've helped people not only buy one home, but several homes, so they could build a wealth portfolio. So they could create financial freedom and legacies for their children and their children's children. That is what purpose will do. It will anoint you in ways that you can't or won't understand.

Your purpose doesn't have to be perfect, or public. Do it, even if it's on a shoestring budget at first. Do it, even if it's in the dark, or just you and one person that you feel an urgency to help. Once God tells you to move, you won't have everything you think you need and you won't know everything you need to know out of the gate. But God wants to know you will trust Him enough to start walking when He tells you to, even though you feel like you're in the dark. Put your hands out in front of you and feel your way through. Follow the feeling.

When God has placed something on the inside of you, in your belly, it's going to happen. That is Him speaking to you. You may not be comfortable, but you will be a peace when you are moving towards your purpose.

Stay the course. And, please, don't give up right before it's your turn to win.

Imagine you are digging for treasure. It may be buried for miles and miles beneath the surface, but you know it's there. After digging for days, you're tired, sweaty, and hungry. Despite what you believe, you ignore what you know, and decide to quit. Little did you know in those next two scoops of dirt, your shovel would have hit the top of that chest filled with gold, diamonds, and precious pearls.

How would you feel?

That is exactly what it would be like to miss out on all that God has for you. Your abundance and overflow gone because you threw the shovel in too soon.

When you know your purpose and understand that it's a GIFT, having that gift is a privilege. Acting on that gift is POWER.

CHAPTER SIX
BREAKING INTO GROWTH, ABUNDANCE, AND OVERFLOW

"God, grant us growth, abundance, and overflow."

For the last five years, I've prayed that prayer for my family, myself, and my business. I'll often come into the office early, go down my agent roster, and petition God for every single person. "God, bless them with growth, abundance, and overflow both in their business and their personal lives."

Those words guide me every day of my life. They are so powerful for me that I have them printed and hanging on the wall of our office so anyone who comes through our doors understands the spiritual energy that we operate in. We are clear about what we are here for. The prayer says it all.

I've attached principles to that prayer that have changed everything for me. Growth, Abundance, and Overflow pour into my life in big and small ways. It comes because I am ready to receive it. I work for it. But most importantly, I pray for it. Once you begin to pray for the same (and I hope you do), here are some practical steps you can take to do get ready for growth, abundance, and overflow in your own life and to do your work to receive it.

Growth

Growth is a constant state of evolving by which you transform mentally, physically, emotionally, and spiritually. If you are not growing, you are stagnant, which means that everything else that is intended for you is on hold until you move to get to it. If you are in the same position at 42 that you were at 22 or even 32, something needs to change.

Evaluate your life. Evaluate your situation, then begin to make changes. The change doesn't have to be enormous or totally life transforming all at once, but make small gradual steps over a period of time. We never get to a place where we've perfected our life, so we should always be seeking to grow in different ways.

Here are small things you can do to accelerate growth in your life:

Limit social media. Limit social media time. Spend more time 'doing' instead of browsing. There are 2.77 billion people on social media. The average user logs on for 135 minutes per day and social media is one of the biggest productivity thieves. For many of us, the first thing we do when we wake up is check our phones. We get an endorphin rush when we see alerts pop up. In our minds, we think we're going to browse just a few minutes, and the next thing we know, that few minutes turns to hours. During the time we are browsing, emails could have been returned, ideas could have been formulated and masterpieces could've been manifested. We could've been much further in accomplishing our God-given dreams. In his book, *Outliers*, Malcolm Gladwell discovered it takes 10,000 hours to master something. If you are the average social media user, you use a good chunk of that in a year.

What would the year have looked like had you spent two hours a day working on your dreams instead of watching other people live theirs?

Pray and meditate. Before you start your day, pray and meditate. Pray a prayer of gratitude thanking God for everything you have, everything you've had, and all the blessings coming your way. Acknowledgment and gratitude will open many opportunities in the universe. It puts you in a position to receive more than you could imagine. You will be blessed with the big things if you are grateful and acknowledge the small ones. If your car isn't acting right, be grateful that you are blessed with the car you have and be thankful for the dream car that's on the horizon. You may not be living in the house you want but be thankful you have a roof over your head and for the beautiful dream home that you will have in the future. Ask for direction on how to make it happen. If your kids aren't acting right, be thankful your kids are alive and safe. Continue to pour into them, love them, and pray for them. Ask for your heart to be continually filled with love and peace. Prayer is talking to God and meditation is receiving the answers. When you meditate, clear your mind and allow God to pour into you. You are getting clarity and understanding. Continue this practice daily, this is key to your growth.

Abundance

Abundance is a holistic experience that is not just about riches or money, but the wealth of blessings in every area of your life. Abundance always begins in the mind. Cultivate these mindsets and watch abundance flow your way.
Freedom Mindset
When you are at one with yourself and at peace with your God, your mind is clear, and the possibilities are endless. I would much rather have freedom of mind than any amount of riches in the world. When your mind is free, you can accomplish ANYthing! The million-dollar ideas start to take shape. The path to get there

becomes clear, and the confidence to execute becomes attainable. Freedom and clarity of mind are some of the biggest blessings you can have in your life.

Wealth Mindset
When it comes to financial abundance, you must have the mindset for it. Your words have to line up with the things you know to be true. Words are powerful. Words are prophetic. Words are key. Broke, lack, and scarcity can't dwell in the same space as growth, abundance, and overflow. They're completely opposite. It's like basic math—a negative times a positive equal a negative. You will never bring any wealth into your hands if you are not open to receive it. Speak positivity. Save your resources. Avoid negativity at all costs.

Gracious Mindset
Abundance comes to those who are optimistic and are genuinely happy for others when they achieve success. Scarcity will cause you to feel competitive and resent others' wins. You'll only see the negative and never the positive, for yourself or anyone else. But as you begin to focus on living in gratitude and your mind is free, your conversations will begin to change. Broke,

brokenness, fear, lack, harm, and hate will have no place in your spirit or in your conversation. Speak life, freedom, hope, happiness, positivity, possibilities, love, and light.

Overflow

Living in overflow is not just about the having, it is also about the giving. And it's not giving because you have, it's giving because it's in your spirit to do so. Gandhi said the best way to find yourself is to lose yourself in the giving. Giving isn't always monetary. It's your time, your talent, and your treasure.

What are you willing to give to others above and beyond the norm? What I know for sure is that when your hands are extended to give, you are also in a position to receive.

Your Time – Time is the biggest commodity we have. We all have the same 24 hours in the day, but what we do with our time is what matters most. Taking time to give back will not only help others, but it will give you peace and fulfillment.

Your Talent – When you are blessed with a gift, don't keep it to yourself, share it! Your gift will make room for you, and if on occasion you gift your gift, you will see a ten-fold return.

Your Treasure – Where your treasure is, your heart will be also. What do you treasure most?

Whatever it is, sacrificing it at times will ensure that your treasure never runs dry.

For a long time, I used to say, "God, you don't have to make me an example in order for me to learn."

I know now that what I was really asking for was a way out. I didn't want to feel what it was like to lose. I had struggled so much in my life, and I wanted God to know that I got it. Enough already. I didn't need to go through anymore hard things to understand what not to do anymore.

"I'll take it from here," was what my words must have sounded like to Him.

Do I need to tell you that didn't work?

He continued to reset me. He kept showing me, teaching me, repositioning me, all through loss, failure, and brokenness. He reminded me that I was made for something more. Had I not lost, had I not been broken, I never would have had a chance to win. And those losses and those wins are why I am here, to share and to guide you through and towards some of the biggest breakthroughs of your life. Trust me, these words won't be the last you hear from me. We're in this thing, together. This is just the beginning of our movement to move our entire community from scarcity to success, from wanting wealth, and in position to create lives worth living and legacies worth creating. It is no coincidence that we've been in this country for 400 years. Like the children of Israel who were enslaved in bondage for 400 years before they were awakened and set free. Our time in bondage is over. We are moving to our Promised Land. And we're going to do it together.

We are all here to learn, but we're also here to lead. So many of us are moving through this world still broken, in our minds, money, and belief. Once we master the principles, once we break The CODE, we have a responsibility to go back and get anyone else who is still stuck in the struggle. What we didn't get coming into and through this world as children, we can give to each other now. We do that so that our children and our grandchildren and the generations to follow won't have to wonder what wealth feels like. They will wake up in it—as they were created to do. We have to make that happen for them. But, first, we need to make it happen for ourselves.

I talk and teach money and wealth principles a lot, but I am not here to just to preach prosperity. I am here to preach possibility. I am here to preach purpose. I am here to preach passion. I am here to be your mirror, to show you how someone who can start out broken can become whole. I'm just a few generations from slavery, I grew up in a home of love, chaos, and abandonment. I am a little girl from San Jose with big dreams who was willing to take big risks. A girl who believed in herself beyond anything rational or reasonable. I became a woman who was open to walking into unchartered territory, even while she was shaking in her stilettos. You can create success far beyond anything you thought possible. I thought that success would be a small, simple home, a loving wonderful husband, great kids that I could afford daycare for, and a good job with benefits. That was my vision. That was success to me. And God gave me what I asked for, all while planting a seed in me for more. He supersized my success, and He's still opening doors. So when you see me, see yourself. See what is possible when you become obsessed— and obedient.

I have given you a blueprint to success in this book, based on some things that have worked for me and I know, given openness, time, and lots of sweat equity, will work for you, too. Putting these principles into practice will certainly shorten your learning curve, but that doesn't mean that you will avoid every mistake. I can certainly help you to avoid some, but neither I, nor no one else, can show you how to circumvent them all. The best lessons are the ones that come the hardest. But I will say that guides like me and other people who have walked this walk before you can help you to get up when you fall, to bounce back and be better than you were before. If I can leave you with nothing else, it's this: Claim what you deserve. Boldly and unapologetically. It doesn't matter if you are the first, and only, person you know to ever do it or have it.

Understand that wealth is not a far-fetched possibility for people who get lucky. Wealth is for people who are in position and on purpose. Figure out ways to not blow your money so you can grow your money.

Seek out spaces that scare you that are filled with people who have more than you, or who are moving in the direction that you are trying to go in.

Create something.

Oh, and one more thing.

Break free.

CHAPTER SEVEN
BREAKING THE MINDSET TO GOAL SET

I've spent years studying what it takes to be successful. I believe in following the paths of people who have done it well before me, so I look to high-achieving, "won't stop" people in the world who refuse to give up on their dreams, and they've reaped rewards as a result.

One of the common practices of ridiculous success is the Law of Attraction. I encourage you to read more about it on your own, and choose to apply the practice to your own life. It connects to so much that we've talked about already— particularly believing in yourself and speaking your prayers as though they already are. When you open yourself up to receive what you want, it will come.

Use these simple steps to begin to evoke the power of attraction into your life:

Think it – "Whatever the mind can conceive and believe, it can achieve with positive mental attitude." —Napoleon Hill. Close your eyes and think about what you want to do. Think about the end result. How would your life change because of it? What would it do for your family? What would it do for your legacy? Your life will never change if you have no vision for it. "Where there is no vision, the people perish" (Proverbs 29:18).

Close your eyes and think about what you want to do. Think about the end result. How would your life change because of it? What would it do for your family? What would it do for your legacy? Your life will never change if you have no vision for it.

Assignment: Get quiet and still for as long as you need, and visualize what your life *will* look like one year from now. Then two years. Then five years.

Write it – There is something very powerful about writing down your goals. Once you've determined what your goal is, put together your to-do list. Work your plan and watch those things come into fruition. My goals are written in my phone, so they are with me everywhere I go. At any given time, I can look at them and be reminded of the things I need to accomplish based on my goals. Your goals can evolve as you do, they don't have to stay the same. Be open to the possibilities. "Write down the vision and make it plain" (Habakkuk 2:2).

Assignment: Write down your vision, goals, and plan.

Vision

_____
_____
_____
_____
_____
_____
_____
_____
_____
_____
_____
_____
_____
_____
_____
_____
_____
_____

Goals

_____
_____
_____
_____
_____
_____

Plan

_____

_____

Speak it – Your goals should become your affirmations—say them out loud every day. Summon your life, success, health, and wealth into existence. When you put words into the universe, energy begins to move into the atmosphere and your desires begin to manifest in your life. You have to speak life over your goals. When I am obsessed with something, every morning before I go to the gym, I review my goals and read them out loud. I can feel things beginning to shift in my favor and it motivates me to take action. "Life and death are in the power of the tongue" (Proverbs 18:21).

Assignment: Speak your goals out loud.
Example – *I will make $90,000 by the end of next year.*

Work it – Plan the work and work the plan. Thinking, writing, and speaking are the vehicle, but doing the work is the fuel to get you to your destination. That means researching, networking, investing, and good old-fashioned hard work. Whatever your goal is, you must be willing to eat, drink, sleep, breathe, and live it daily. Your drive and tenacity are the icing on the cake. "Faith without works is dead" (James 2:14).

<u>Assignment</u>: Map out the specific work you need to do to reach your goals.
The training I will take to ensure I reach my goals is:

_____
_____
_____
_____

The connections I will make to ensure I reach my goals are:

_____
_____
_____
_____
_____

I will work _____ extra hours on my business.
I am committed to getting a mentor within the next _____ months to help me navigate my journey to success.

Receive it – By committing to the four steps above, you can manifest your dreams. Dreams don't come easy and there is no overnight success, but there is definitely a formula for it and if you follow it, you will manifest it. "Don't be weary in well doing, for in due season you will reap your harvest" (Galatians 6:9).

Keep track of your wins along the way. They don't have to be gigantic. Celebrate both the big and small.

_____

_____

_____

_____

_____

_____

_____

_____

_____

_____

_____

_____

_____

_____

_____

_____

_____

_____

_____

ACKNOWLEDGEMENTS

As I stated before, I am truly grateful to have an amazing village of support around me. Especially my rock, and biggest supporter my loving husband Warren Carter, whom I've loved since my teenage years. Together we have managed to build quite a life of adventure while manifesting our dreams. I truly love and appreciate you. My daughter Chayil, my first heartbeat, you my love, have made my life complete. I see so much beauty inside of you. You are loving, caring and unique. You're my very best friend. Thank you for being my ride or die. To my son Warren Jr., I so love your heart. You are a true leader, a great big brother, an excellent son and an amazing friend. Thank you for keeping me on the straight and narrow. My son Kyren (aka my Little Middle), the quiet storm. From the day you were born, you had a quiet and calming spirit. You, my son, are my nurturer. You're always taking care of me and fixing things around the house. You are indeed the triple threat – brains, athlete, and musician. Thank you for exemplifying what it means to be a King. My baby boy Kamil. The meaning of your name says it all. You truly complete our family. You bring such a light and joy in our home & our lives. You've always been a little comedian and you keep us entertained and on our toes. You are the consummate musician and baby of the family, and the only one who will still let me kiss him. Thank you for being Mommy's constant affection. It's now no secret that I use to secretly tell each of you that you were all my favorite, and you all believed me until you started comparing notes. Lol. You all love your parents so much, but what I'm most proud about is how much you love one another.

I'm so thankful for the relationship I have with my parents. We have quite a village. My dad has since remarried and my dad, mom, and his current wife are all besties. It's a beautiful thing to witness. They all come together, along with my mother-in-law, and are the best grandparents ever. Thank you, Mom & Dad, for the constant support you show and the love you continue to give. My brothers & sister are the best. Thank you for our close bond, love, and mutual respect. RIP to my father-in-law Thomas. You too, were a great Grandpa to our children.

I would be remiss if I didn't mention my partner in crime Glenda who has worked for me since 2007. You have been there through all the ups and downs, the famine and the feast. You, my friend, inspire me to think bigger. I am grateful, and truly appreciate who you are in my life, Glenda. Oprah said, "Lots of people want to ride with you in the limo, but you want someone who will take the bus with you when the limo breaks down". Glenda, you have truly been that and so much more for me.

The change agents of Catalyst Real Estate Professionals, thank you for pouring into me and allowing me to pour into you. You all are truly my superpower. You were hand selected by God for greatness. Continue to do great work in the community.

To all of my friends and family that hold me down, support me, and believe in me... Thank you. Your love and prayers sustain me.

Dear God,

Thank you for a blessed and magical life!

~Constance

MEET THE AUTHOR

Constance Carter is an International Best-Selling Author, Investor, Speaker, Musician and the CEO of the largest African American Residential Real Estate & Lending firm in Northern California. Her books include O.N.E, Build Credit to Build Wealth, Keeping Score and latest release, The Secret to Breaking the B.R.O.K.E Code. She has been featured in several publications including The Huffington Post, Black Enterprise, Rolling Out Magazine, Thrive Global, and Fox News. Constance also serves as a Speaker Advocate Coach for International Speaker, Lisa Nichols & Motivating the Masses. Between running her successful real estate firm, speaking, her training programs, media appearances, in addition to having a busy family of 6, she truly lives her motto, Nobody Works Harder than Constance Carter.

Websites:
constancecarter.com
mywealthroadmap.com
catalystrealestate.com

Social Media
www.facebook.com/constancecarterbroker
Instagram @constancedenisecarter
Twitter @askconstancec
LinkedIn – linkedin.com/in/constancecarter

CONSTANCE
CARTER